Pride Prejudice and *Parties*

© Copyright Leviticus Ltd 2024
© Copyright R.Thomas
All rights reserved.

The content contained within this book may not be reproduced, duplicated, or transmitted without direct written permission from the author or the publisher.

The information provided within this book is for entertainment purposes only. While the author has made every effort to ensure the accuracy and completeness of the information contained in this book, the author and publisher assume no responsibility for errors, omissions, or contrary interpretations of the subject matter herein. Under no circumstances will any blame or legal responsibility be held against the publisher, or author, for any damages, reparation, or monetary loss due to the information contained within this book, either directly or indirectly.

Contents

Introduction　2

Would You Rather　4
Players are presented with humorous and thought-provoking dilemmas inspired by Pride and Prejudice or the Regency Era.

Regency Charades　16
Charades with a Regency twist!

Pride and Prejudice Trivia　20
A trivia game where players answer questions about the characters, plot, and Regency-era customs.

Match the Quote　26
Players are given a selection of quotes from Pride and Prejudice and must match them to the character who said them.

Genteel Gibberish Translations　30
In this game of Regency translations, players reinterpret modern scenarios into the eloquent language of the Regency era, adding a touch of wit and charm to everyday mishaps.

Afternoon Tea Cookoff　34
Embark on a delightful afternoon of culinary competition, where scones rise like eager suitors and sandwiches whisper secrets of taste and tradition, all amidst the charm and wit of a Regency-era tea party worthy of Miss Jane Austen's keen observation.

Regency Recipes　39
Partake in a culinary journey through time, where each recipe embodies the elegance of a bygone era, promising a feast of flavours to delight even the most discerning of palates.

As a small thank you for buying this book, here's a Pride and Prejudice surprise for you to enjoy!
Just scan this QR code!

Welcome, Dear Reader, to a Regency Revelry Like No Other!

Step into the world of Jane Austen with "Pride and Prejudice and Parties: Regency Era Entertainment for Austen Enthusiasts."

This book is your ultimate guide to hosting Pride and Prejudice-themed parties and gatherings. Whether you're planning a cosy night in or a grand Regency-inspired soirée, it's bursting with games, activities, and ideas to transport you and your guests back to the enchanting world of Elizabeth Bennet, Mr Darcy, and the charming countryside estates of 19th-century England.

From lively games of "Would You Rather" to elegant Regency charades, there's something for every Austen aficionado to enjoy. So, dust off your dancing shoes, practice your curtsies and bows, and prepare to immerse yourself in a world of romance, intrigue, and social grace.

Whether you're a long-time Janeite or a newcomer to the world of Austen, "Pride and Prejudice and Parties" promises hours of entertainment, laughter, and the chance to experience the magic of Regency England from the comfort of your own home.

So, let the games begin, and may your parties be as delightful as a walk through the gardens of Pemberley!

Would You Rather?

INSTRUCTIONS:

This game is best enjoyed in the company of friends and fellow Austen enthusiasts, with someone to act as the host, presenting each "Would You Rather" dilemma in turn. Players are urged to go turn by turn, choosing what they would rather do and explaining their choice. Laughter, debate, and witty banter are encouraged!

Would you rather attend the Netherfield ball wearing a dress that's a decade out of fashion or not be invited at all?

Imagine the gasps and whispers of Meryton's finest as you make your grand entrance. Will you risk the fashion faux pas or sacrifice the pleasure of Mr. Bingley's company?
The choice is yours, and the consequences, oh, so entertaining!

Would you rather have Mrs. Bennet as your mother or Mr. Collins as your clergyman?

Ah, the joys of familial relations and romantic guidance in the village of Meryton! Would you prefer the incessant matchmaking endeavours of Mrs. Bennet or the tedious sermons and sycophantic flattery of Mr. Collins? A challenging decision indeed!

Would you rather dance with Mr. Wickham and risk a scandal or sit out the dance entirely?

The allure of Mr. Wickham's charming demeanour is undeniable, but at what cost? Will you risk the scandalous whispers of society or forego the pleasure of the dance altogether? Choose wisely, for reputations are delicate things in Regency England!

Would you rather accept the initial proposal of Mr. Collins or Mr. Darcy?

Ah, the pivotal moment of matrimony! Would you choose the socially advantageous but utterly awkward proposal of Mr. Collins, with his rambling compliments? Or perhaps you'd prefer the proud and haughty declaration from Mr. Darcy, whose initial offer was fraught with offence and misunderstanding?

Would you rather visit Rosings Park with Lady Catherine de Bourgh as your hostess or spend a day with the obsequious Mr. Collins?

Imagine the grandeur of Rosings Park under the scrutinizing eye of Lady Catherine de Bourgh! Or perhaps you'd prefer the company of Mr. Collins, with his effusive compliments and ceaseless deference. A day of condescension either way—what say you?

Would you rather be a guest at Pemberley during Mr. Darcy's absence or endure a rainy day at Longbourn with the entire Bennet family?

Two contrasting settings beckon: the elegance of Pemberley, shrouded in the absence of its master, or the lively chaos of Longbourn on a rainy day. Where would you rather find yourself, dear reader?

Would you rather be Charlotte Lucas' younger sister, Maria, or Lydia Bennet?

Would you choose the prudent and practical life of Maria Lucas, destined for a quiet existence as the companion to her whimsical father? Or perhaps the giddy and flirtatious nature of Lydia Bennet, always seeking excitement and attention? A sisterly dilemma indeed!

Would you rather have Mr. Bingley as your best friend but risk his indecisiveness or Mr. Darcy as your friend but deal with his initial arrogance?

The delightful Mr. Bingley with his sunny disposition, yet plagued by indecision, or the enigmatic Mr. Darcy, proud and aloof, yet possessing hidden depths? Friendship in Regency society is not without its challenges!

Would you rather receive advice on love and marriage from Mr. Bennet or Mrs. Bennet?

Seeking counsel on matters of the heart? Will you turn to the witty and detached observations of Mr. Bennet or the fervent and misguided enthusiasm of Mrs. Bennet? Choose your advisor wisely, for the path to matrimony is fraught with peril and passion!

Would you rather be the recipient of a fashion critique from Caroline Bingley or a lecture on the merits of sensible footwear from Charlotte Lucas?

Will you withstand Caroline Bingley's relentless pursuit of fashion perfection, enduring her exacting standards and snobbish commentary? Or will you graciously accept Charlotte Lucas' well-meaning but somewhat unexciting lecture on the merits of sensible footwear?

Would you rather attend an art class to paint Georgiana Darcy or a musical recital featuring Mr Collins' favourite hymns?

Two artistic endeavours beckon! Will you attempt to capture the elegance of Miss Darcy on canvas in a painting class? Or will you endure the solemn melodies of Mr Collins' favourite hymns in a musical recital?

Would you rather be the recipient of a dubious culinary creation by Mrs. Bennet or a tedious lecture on beekeeping from Sir William Lucas?

Will you dare to sample Mrs. Bennet's questionable culinary concoction, prepared with questionable ingredients and even more questionable skill? Or will you patiently endure Sir William Lucas' exhaustive and somewhat tedious discourse on the art and science of beekeeping?

Would you rather be caught in the rain with Mr. Darcy or stranded in the countryside with Mr. Wickham?

Will you find shelter from the rain under Mr. Darcy's protective arm, his brooding charm and steadfast demeanor offering solace from the storm? Or will you navigate the countryside's uncertainties alongside Mr. Wickham, his roguish allure and smooth words tempting fate and testing your judgment?

Would you rather have Caroline Bingley plan your wedding or Mr Collins write your vows?

Will you entrust Caroline Bingley with the orchestration of your wedding, her impeccable taste and high-society standards guiding every detail with an air of refinement and a hint of condescension? Or will you endure the cringe-worthy prose of Mr. Collins as he pens your vows, his obsequious verbosity and misguided attempts at eloquence leaving much to be desired?

Would you rather have the fate of Charlotte Lucas or Lydia Bennet?

Will you opt for the practical path of Charlotte Lucas, choosing security and stability over romantic illusions, and finding contentment in a marriage of convenience? Or will you embrace the heedless impulsiveness of Lydia Bennet, risking reputation and respectability for a reckless romance?

Would you rather attend a ball with mismatched gloves or with a slightly wrinkled gown?

In the world of Regency-era balls, appearance is everything. Will you risk the whispered gossip and disapproving glances that come with mismatched gloves? Or will you endure the subtle discomfort and potential scrutiny of a slightly wrinkled gown? A fashion faux pas or a wrinkle in time?

Would you rather have your carriage break down in the rain on the way to your wedding or trip and fall while walking down the aisle?

Will you brave the elements and potential delays of a broken carriage in the rain on your wedding day? Or will you risk the embarrassment and awkward recovery of tripping and falling while walking down the aisle? A dampened wedding day or a stumbling start to marital bliss?

Would you rather receive a bouquet of wildflowers or a meticulously arranged and expensive bouquet from a florist?

Will you embrace the rustic charm and spontaneity of a bouquet of wildflowers? Or will you delight in the elegance and extravagance of a meticulously arranged and expensive bouquet from a renowned florist? A wild and whimsical gesture or a display of refined taste—which will you choose?

WOULD YOU RATHER BE STUCK IN A CARRIAGE RIDE WITH A TALKATIVE PARROT OR A SNORING PUG AS YOUR ONLY COMPANIONS FOR A JOURNEY TO BATH?

Imagine the scandalous tales the parrot would squawk about, my dear! But then again, the pug's snores might provide a soothing soundtrack for your journey to Bath. Oh, the perils of Regency travel!

WOULD YOU RATHER ATTEND A SOCIETY BALL WHERE EVERYONE IS REQUIRED TO WEAR MISMATCHED SHOES OR A MASQUERADE WHERE THE MASKS ARE ALL UPSIDE DOWN?

Mismatched shoes? How positively daring! Though I must say, an upside-down mask might add an amusing twist to the masquerade, wouldn't you agree? Decisions, decisions, in the realm of Regency fashion faux pas!

WOULD YOU RATHER RECEIVE A MARRIAGE PROPOSAL VIA CARRIER PIGEON OR HAVE YOUR COURTSHIP DOCUMENTED IN A SCANDALOUS NOVEL BY A NOTORIOUS GOSSIP COLUMNIST?

A marriage proposal via carrier pigeon? How delightfully unconventional! But a courtship chronicled in a scandalous novel? The talk of the ton, my dear, but perhaps not in the way one would wish! Oh, the romantic follies of Regency courtship!

Would you rather accidentally address a Prince by his first name or forget the title entirely?

The delicate intricacies of Regency-era etiquette. Will you risk the familiarity and potential offence of addressing a Prince by his first name? Or will you face the embarrassment and potential disrespect of forgetting his title entirely? A misstep in address or a lapse in courtesy—which will you choose?

Would you rather host a dinner party with a surprise menu by a new cook or with a strict adherence to traditional dishes?

Oh, the culinary conundrums of Regency-era entertaining! Will you embrace the adventurous spirit and unpredictability of a surprise menu by a new and untested cook? Or will you opt for the tried-and-true comfort and familiarity of traditional dishes? A culinary gamble or a feast of tradition—which will you choose, dear reader?

Would you rather be invited to an intimate picnic by the lake with your beau or at the Regent's garden party in full bloom?

Will you choose the secluded charm and intimate setting of a picnic by the lake with your beloved? Or will you opt for the grandeur and bustling excitement of the Regent's garden party, where every bloom vies for admiration as much as the whispered scandal?

Would you rather dance with a handsome man who constantly steps on your toes or an average-looking one who never lets go of your hand?

Will you endure the pain of crushed toes in the arms of a dashing but clumsy partner? Or will you navigate the dance floor with an unremarkable but attentive companion? A painful elegance or a comforting constancy—which shall it be, dear reader?

Would you rather be the talk of the town for your impeccable manners or for your scandalous behavior?

Will you be admired and emulated for your flawless grace and impeccable manners, the envy of every drawing room? Or will you become the subject of scandalous gossip, your daring deeds and audacious choices captivating the imagination of the town's most avid gossip-monger? A paragon of propriety or a magnet for mischief—which shall it be?

Would you rather accidentally spill red wine on your host's carpet or break a valuable piece of china?

Will you face the mortifying moment of staining your host's pristine carpet with a splash of red wine, the vivid hue a stark contrast to the decor? Or will you endure the heart-stopping sound of a valuable piece of china shattering at your clumsy touch, the delicate fragments a testament to your unfortunate mishap?

Would you rather wear a hat adorned with peacock feathers or a brightly coloured bonnet embellished with ribbons?

Ah, the flamboyant fashion choices and vibrant vogue of Regency-era headwear! Will you strut with the majestic allure of peacock feathers perched atop your crown, each iridescent plume capturing the eye and igniting envy? Or will you don a bonnet of bold hues, its ribbons dancing in the breeze like playful confetti celebrating your sartorial audacity?

Would you rather have a witty repartee with a charming rogue or a serious conversation with a sensible suitor?

Enticing choices of Regency-era companionship, indeed! Will you be swept away by the playful banter of a charming rogue, his wit as sharp as his intentions are questionable? Or will you engage in a thoughtful and earnest dialogue with a sensible suitor, his conversation as steady as his prospects are promising? A dance of words or a heart-to-heart—which shall it be?

Would you rather be invited to a masked ball or a costume party inspired by Shakespearean characters?

Will you don a mysterious mask, concealing your identity as you dance the night away, your secret allure captivating fellow masked revelers? Or will you embrace the dramatic flair of Shakespearean characters, your costume a tribute to the timeless tales and tragicomedies of the Bard's beloved plays?

Would you rather be serenaded under the balcony or receive a love letter written in verse?

Will you bask in the moonlit serenade, the heartfelt melodies echoing beneath your balcony as your admirer pours out their affection in song? Or will you savour the intimate sentiments penned in verse, each poetic line a testament to your suitor's eloquent adoration? A serenade of song or a verse of passion?

Would you rather be caught in a compromising situation or be accused of spreading scandalous rumors?

Will you face the blush-inducing embarrassment of being caught in a compromising situation, your reputation teetering on the edge of propriety? Or will you bear the weight of scandalous accusations, the sharp tongues of society questioning your honour and integrity? A moment of indiscretion or a cloud of controversy—which do you choose?

Would you rather inherit a family heirloom with sentimental value or a valuable piece of art with a mysterious past?

Will you treasure a family heirloom, its sentimental value a heartwarming reminder of ancestors past and cherished memories? Or will you be captivated by a valuable piece of art, its enigmatic past shrouded in mystery and intrigue, each brushstroke whispering tales of bygone days?

Regency Charades

INSTRUCTIONS:

The Host divides players into two teams. The first team selects a performer to act out the phrase without speaking. The performer draws a piece of paper from the prepared stack (by the host) and secretly reads the phrase, then acts it out while their team members try to guess what it is within a time limit, typically one to two minutes. The performer can use gestures, facial expressions, and body language to convey the phrase, but cannot make any noises or speak.

If the team correctly guesses before time runs out, they earn a point. If the team is unable to guess correctly within the time limit, play passes to the other team, who then selects a performer for their turn. Each correctly guessed phrase earns one point for the performing team. The game concludes when either one team reaches the predetermined winning score or after the set number of rounds.

CHARADE PROMPTS

- Mr. Collins clumsily attempting to impress the Bennet family during his visit to Longbourn.
- Lydia and Kitty Bennet giggling and gossiping together about the officers and their uniforms.
- Elizabeth Bennet teasing Mr. Darcy with playful banter and witty retorts.
- Mr. Bingley nervously seeking Mr. Darcy's approval before proposing to Jane Bennet.
- Lady Catherine de Bourgh interrogating Elizabeth Bennet about her family background and connections.
- Charlotte Lucas advising Elizabeth on the practicalities of marriage and securing her future.
- Mr. Wickham charming the ladies with his smooth manners and charming smile.
- Mrs. Bennet scheming to matchmake her daughters with eligible bachelors at the local assemblies.
- Mr. Darcy awkwardly attempting to dance with Elizabeth at the Netherfield ball.
- Jane Bennet gracefully enduring Mrs. Hurst and Miss Bingley's snide comments and condescension.
- Mr. Collins obsequiously complimenting Lady Catherine de Bourgh on her exquisite taste and generosity.
- Elizabeth Bennet receiving Mr. Collins' proposal with a mix of disbelief and amusement.

- Elizabeth Bennet discovering Mr. Darcy's letter and grappling with conflicting emotions as she reads it.
- Mr. Bennet quipping sarcastically to his wife in response to her constant fretting and matchmaking efforts.
- Mary Bennet earnestly attempting to engage Mr. Collins in a discussion on moral philosophy.
- Georgiana Darcy shyly observing the social interactions at a gathering, her innocence and reserve endearing her to others.
- Mr. Collins delivering a tedious and long-winded sermon to the Bennet family during his visit to Longbourn.
- Caroline Bingley attempting to undermine Jane Bennet's prospects with Mr. Bingley through subtle manipulation and deceit.
- Mr. Darcy overcoming his pride and prejudice to publicly declare his love for Elizabeth in a grand romantic gesture.
- Mrs. Bennet proudly boasting about the accomplishments and connections of her daughters to anyone who will listen.
- Elizabeth Bennet boldly standing up to Lady Catherine de Bourgh and asserting her independence and worth.
- Mr. Darcy delivering his first proposal to Elizabeth, filled with awkwardness and sincerity.

- Caroline Bingley attempting to attract Mr. Darcy's attention with subtle (or not-so-subtle) flirtation.
- Mr. Collins fawning over Lady Catherine and seeking her approval at every turn.
- Charlotte Lucas agreeing to marry Mr. Collins for practical reasons, despite her lack of affection for him.
- Mr. Wickham spinning tall tales of his exploits and misfortunes to anyone who will listen.
- Mrs. Bennet fretting over the possibility of her daughters becoming old maids.
- Mr. Collins boasting about the grandeur of his patroness, Lady Catherine de Bourgh.
- Mary Bennet attempting to impress others with her knowledge and musical skills at the Netherfield ball.
- Mr. Bennet retreating to his library to escape the chaos of his household and the incessant chatter of his wife.
- Mr. Darcy and Elizabeth sharing a meaningful glance across a crowded room, hinting at their growing attraction despite their differences.
- Lydia Bennet flirting shamelessly with the officers at the Meryton assembly.
- Mr. Bingley professing his love to Jane Bennet with earnestness and affection.
- Mrs. Bennet gossiping with her neighbors about potential suitors for her daughters.

Pride and Prejudice Trivia

INSTRUCTIONS:

Each team shall appoint a captain to lead them through the challenges of Regency-era knowledge. As the host asks questions, take turns answering with the elegance and wit befitting a true Austen aficionado.

Collaboration and camaraderie are encouraged, for in the end, it is the joy of shared knowledge and laughter that truly prevails.

Let the game commence, and may the best team revel in the glory of victory!

Pride & Prejudice Trivia

Question: What is the name of the Bennet family estate?
Answer: Longbourn.

Question: Who is the eldest Bennet sister?
Answer: Jane Bennet.

Question: What is the occupation of Mr. Bennet?
Answer: He is a gentleman farmer.

Question: What is Mr. Darcy's first name?
Answer: Fitzwilliam.

Question: What is the name of Mr. Darcy's estate?
Answer: Pemberley.

Question: Who is the middle Bennet sister?
Answer: Mary Bennet.

Question: What is the name of Mr. Darcy's aunt who disapproves of Elizabeth?
Answer: Lady Catherine de Bourgh.

Question: What is the name of the Bennet family housekeeper?
Answer: Mrs. Hill.

Question: Who is the militia officer who elopes with Lydia Bennet?
Answer: George Wickham.

Question: What is the name of Mr. Darcy's sister?
Answer: Georgiana.

Question: What is the name of the street where the Gardiners reside in London?
Answer: Gracechurch Street.

Question: What is the name of Mr. Darcy's housekeeper at Pemberley?
Answer: Mrs. Reynolds.

Question: What is the first name of Mr. Gardiner, Elizabeth Bennet's uncle?
Answer: Edward

Question: What is the name of the town where the Bennet family resides?
Answer: Meryton.

Question: What is the name of Mr. Bingley's brother-in-law?
Answer: Mr. Hurst.

Question: What is the name of the estate where Mr. Darcy's aunt, Lady Catherine de Bourgh, resides?
Answer: Rosings Park.

Question: What is the first name of Mrs Bennet?
Answer: Fanny.

Question: What was Jane Austen's original title for Pride and Prejudice?
Answer: First Impressions.

Question: How many marriages occur in the course of the novel?
Answer: 5 - those of Colonel Forster, Mr Collins, Wickham, Bingley, and Darcy.

Question: In the 1995 BBC TV adaptation Darcy accidentally meets Elizabeth as he emerges from a swim in Pemberley lake. But where do they meet in the novel?
Answer: As he comes from the stables.

Question: When did the BBC first broadcast an adaptation of Pride and Prejudice?
Answer: 1924.

Question: Which is 'the place to get husbands' according to Lydia?
Answer: Brighton.

Question: Who played the first on-screen Elizabeth Bennet?
Answer: Greer Garson.

Question: Who is the tallest Bennet sister?
Answer: Lydia Bennet.

Question: In what month did Mr. Darcy first propose to Elizabeth only to be refused?
Answer: April.

Question: Who portrayed Mr. Darcy in the 2005 film adaptation of "Pride and Prejudice"?
Answer: Matthew Macfadyen.

Question: In the 1995 BBC TV series adaptation, who played the role of Elizabeth Bennet?
Answer: Jennifer Ehle.

Question: Who portrayed Lady Catherine de Bourgh in the 2005 film adaptation?
Answer: Dame Judi Dench.

Regency Era Trivia

What was considered the proper way for a gentleman to address a lady during the Regency era?
Answer: "Miss" or "Mrs." followed by her last name.

What was the standard greeting when meeting someone during the Regency era?
Answer: A bow for gentlemen and a curtsy for ladies.

True or False: During the Regency era, it was customary for gentlemen to walk on the outside of the sidewalk when accompanying a lady.
Answer: True.

What item was considered essential for a gentleman to carry when attending a ball or social event during the Regency era?
Answer: A snuffbox.

What was the proper way for a lady to decline a dance invitation during a Regency-era ball?
Answer: Politely decline by saying she is already engaged for that set.

True or False: It was considered improper for a lady to enter a room unaccompanied during the Regency era.
Answer: True.

What was the primary purpose of a Regency-era fan?
Answer: To communicate messages or emotions discreetly.

What item was commonly used by gentlemen to signify their rank or affiliation during the Regency era?
Answer: A cravat pin.

What was the proper way for a gentleman to offer a lady refreshments during a social gathering in the Regency era?
Answer: By asking if she would care for a glass of wine or a cup of tea.

What was the customary length of a morning visit during the Regency era?
Answer: Approximately 15-20 minutes.

What was the primary purpose of a Regency-era calling card?
Answer: To formally request or acknowledge a social visit.

True or False: It was customary for ladies to wear gloves at all times when in public during the Regency era.
Answer: True.

What was the traditional mealtime for dinner during the Regency era?
Answer: Dinner was normally eaten between 6 - 8pm, but this depended on where you lived and your social status.

What was the proper way for a gentleman to offer a lady his seat during the Regency era?
Answer: By standing up and offering the chair with his right hand.

True or False: During the Regency era, it was considered inappropriate for a lady to initiate a conversation with a gentleman.
Answer: True.

What name was often used to describe high society during the Regency era?
Answer: The Ton.

Match the Quote

INSTRUCTIONS:

Gather in two teams for 'Match the Quote,' a Pride and Prejudice-inspired game!

Appoint a host to present quotes; teams match each quote to the character who spoke it. Teams get a point if they get it right, and lose a point if they get it wrong.

Laugh and debate as you vie for victory!

"Next to being married, a girl likes to be crossed a little in love now and then. It is something to think of, and it gives her a sort of distinction among her companions."
ANSWER: Mr. Bennet

"Do anything rather than marry without affection."
ANSWER: Jane Bennet

"There are very few who have heart enough to be really in love without encouragement."
ANSWER: Charlotte Lucas

"You showed me how insufficient were all my pretensions to please a woman worthy of being pleased."
ANSWER: Mr. Darcy

"I think you are in very great danger of making him as much in love with you as ever."
ANSWER: Elizabeth Bennet

"Happiness in marriage is entirely a matter of chance."
ANSWER: Charlotte Lucas

"In vain I have struggled. It will not do. My feelings will no longer be repressed. You must allow me to tell you how ardently I admire and love you."
ANSWER: Mr. Darcy

"A lady's imagination is very rapid; it jumps from admiration to love, from love to matrimony in a moment."
ANSWER: Mr. Darcy

"It is very often nothing but our own vanity that deceives us."
ANSWER: Jane Bennet

"Vanity and pride are different things, though the words are often used synonymously. A person may be proud without being vain. Pride relates more to our opinion of ourselves, vanity to what we would have others think of us."
ANSWER: Mary Bennet

"Nothing is more deceitful... than the appearance of humility."
ANSWER: Mr. Darcy

"I am only resolved to act in that manner, which will, in my own opinion, constitute my happiness, without reference to you, or to any person so wholly unconnected with me."
ANSWER: Elizabeth Bennet

"I am the happiest creature in the world. Perhaps other people have said so before, but not one with such justice."
ANSWER: Elizabeth Bennet

"I declare after all there is no enjoyment like reading! How much sooner one tires of anything than of a book! When I have a house of my own, I shall be miserable if I have not an excellent library."
ANSWER: Caroline Bingley

"I have been so fortunate as to be distinguished by the patronage of the Right Honourable Lady Catherine de Bourgh"
ANSWER: Mr. Collins

"If she is really headstrong and foolish, I know not whether she would altogether be a very desirable wife to a man in my situation."
ANSWER: Mr. Collins

"If I had ever learnt, I should have been a great proficient."
ANSWER: Lady Catherine de Bourgh

"Pray, Miss Eliza, are not the -shire militia removed from Meryton? They must be a great loss to your family."
ANSWER: Caroline Bingley

"What do you think of my husband? Is not he a charming man? I am sure my sisters must all envy me. I only hope they may have half my good luck. They must all go to Brighton. That is the place to get husbands."
ANSWER: Lydia Bennet

"He is as fine a fellow as ever I saw. He simpers, and smirks, and makes love to us all. I am prodigiously proud of him. I defy even Sir William Lucas himself to produce a more valuable son-in-law."
ANSWER: Mr. Bennet

"The world is blinded by his fortune and consequence, or frightened by his high and imposing manners, and sees him only as he chooses to be seen."
ANSWER: George Wickham

"Do not give way to useless alarm, though it is right to be prepared for the worst, there is no occasion to look on it as certain."
ANSWER: Mr. Gardiner

Genteel Gibberish Translations

INSTRUCTIONS:

Gather in two teams for 'Genteel Gibberish,' a game inspired by the delightful wit of Jane Austen's era!

Divide players into teams and designate a Translator for each team's turn, who secretly reads a modern phrase and translates it into faux Austenian language for their team to guess. There's a sample translation in case the player is stuck for words. Team members listen to the translation and collaborate to guess the original modern phrase. Teams earn points for correctly guessing phrases. Rotate the Translator role within each team.

The team with the most points at the end wins the game!

"I accidentally sat on my glasses and broke them in half."
Regency Translation: "Alas, in a moment of carelessness, I placed my spectacles in a precarious position, and upon seating myself, inadvertently fractured them into two distinct pieces."

"I tried to make a fancy dinner for my date and ended up setting off the smoke alarm."
Regency Translation: "In an attempt to prepare an elegant repast for my companion, I inadvertently caused such a commotion in the kitchen that the very apparatus meant to warn of danger was set into motion."

"I accidentally locked myself out of my car with the engine still running."
Regency Translation: "By some misfortune, I found myself stranded outside my carriage with the motive force still engaged, a situation of the most perplexing nature."

"I accidentally left my phone in the refrigerator and spent hours searching for it."
Regency Translation: "In a moment of distraction, I deposited my handheld communication device within the cooling chamber, only to spend countless hours in pursuit of its whereabouts."

"I tried to fix a leaky faucet and ended up flooding the entire bathroom."
Regency Translation: "In my attempt to rectify a leak in the water conduit, I inadvertently exacerbated the situation to such an extent that the entirety of the bathing chamber was inundated with water."

"I tried to bake a cake from scratch and ended up burning it to a crisp."
Regency Translation: "In my endeavour to concoct a confectionery delight from raw ingredients, I regrettably allowed the cake to remain in the oven beyond its appointed time, resulting in a charred and inedible creation."

"I accidentally put my shirt on inside out and didn't realize until halfway through the day."
Regency Translation: "By some oversight, I donned my garment in a manner contrary to convention, discovering my error only after the passage of many hours."

"I tried to parallel park and ended up bumping into the car behind me."
Regency Translation: "In my attempt to maneuver my carriage into a confined space, I inadvertently made contact with the conveyance behind me, a mishap of the most embarrassing nature."

"I tripped over my own feet while walking down the stairs and tumbled to the bottom."
Regency Translation: "Alas, in my descent down the staircase, I became entangled in mine own limbs, resulting in a most undignified descent to the lower landing."

"I accidentally sent a text complaining about my boss to my boss instead of my friend."
Regency Translation: "In a moment of absent-mindedness, I dispatched a missive of complaint regarding my employer to the very person in question, instead of the intended recipient."

"I accidentally wore mismatched shoes to work today."
Regency Translation: "By some oversight, I adorned my feet with footwear of differing design and hue, a fashion faux pas of the most egregious nature."

"I got locked out of my house because I forgot my keys inside."
Regency Translation: "Alas, I found myself stranded outside mine own abode, for I had inadvertently left my means of ingress within, a predicament of the most vexing sort."

"I tried to cut my own hair and ended up with a lopsided haircut."
Regency Translation: "In a moment of folly, I endeavoured to trim mine own locks, resulting in a coiffure of uneven proportions and disarray."

"I accidentally spilled coffee all over my laptop and now it won't turn on."
Regency Translation: "By some misfortune, I overturned my morning libation upon my portable writing desk, rendering it inoperative and bereft of function."

"I mistook my neighbour's dog for a stray and tried to take it home."
Regency Translation: "In a case of mistaken identity, I presumed my neighbour's canine companion to be a wayward vagabond, and attempted to convey it to my own domicile in a misguided act of charity."

Afternoon Tea Cookoff:

INSTRUCTIONS:

Set the Date and Time: Choose a date and time for the cookoff, to align with the tradition of afternoon tea. Encourage guests to dress in Regency-era attire to add to the ambience.

Assign Categories: Participants can choose which category they'd like to compete in and get the ingredients ready such as "Scones," "Tea Sandwiches," "Pastries," and "Sweets."

Cooking and Baking: On the day of the cookoff, participants will cook and bake their chosen items.

Presentation: Each participant should present their creations in a visually appealing manner, similar to how they would be served at a Regency-era afternoon tea.

Tasting and Judging: Set up a designated area for tasting and judging. Guests can sample each item and vote for their favourites in each category.

Award Ceremony: After tasting and judging, announce the winners in each category and award prizes, e.g. ribbons or certificates.

Enjoy the Tea: After the winners are announced, guests can enjoy the delicious spread of Regency-era afternoon tea treats together.

Scones:

Ingredients:

2 cups all-purpose flour
1/4 cup granulated sugar
1 tablespoon baking powder
1/2 teaspoon salt
1/3 cup unsalted butter, chilled and diced
1/2 cup milk
1 large egg
Optional: 1/2 cup raisins or currants

Instructions:

- Preheat the oven to 400°F (200°C). Line a baking sheet with parchment paper.
- In a large bowl, whisk together the flour, sugar, baking powder, and salt.
- Cut in the butter using a pastry cutter or fork until the mixture resembles coarse crumbs.
- In a separate bowl, whisk together the milk and egg. Pour into the dry ingredients and stir until just combined.
- Fold in the raisins or currants, if using.
- Turn the dough out onto a lightly floured surface and knead gently a few times until smooth.
- Pat the dough into a circle about 1 inch thick. Use a biscuit cutter to cut out rounds and place them on the prepared baking sheet.
- Bake for 12-15 minutes or until golden brown. Serve warm with clotted cream and jam.

Tea Sandwiches

Ingredients:

Thinly sliced bread (white or whole wheat)
Assorted fillings such as cucumber, smoked salmon, egg salad, or chicken salad
Softened butter or cream cheese

Instructions:

- Trim the crusts from the bread slices, if desired.
- Spread a thin layer of softened butter or cream cheese on each slice of bread.
- Arrange the fillings evenly on half of the bread slices.
- Top with the remaining bread slices to form sandwiches.
- Use a sharp knife to cut each sandwich into desired shapes, such as triangles or rectangles.
- Arrange the sandwiches on a decorative platter and serve.

Pastries

Ingredients for Raspberry Tarts:

1 sheet puff pastry, thawed
1/2 cup raspberry jam
Fresh raspberries for garnish
Powdered sugar for dusting

Instructions:

- Preheat the oven to 400°F (200°C). Line a baking sheet with parchment paper.
- Roll out the puff pastry sheet on a lightly floured surface.
- Use a round cookie cutter to cut out circles of pastry. Place them on the prepared baking sheet.
- Use a smaller round cutter to make an indentation in the center of each pastry circle, being careful not to cut all the way through.
- Spoon raspberry jam into the center indentation of each pastry circle.
- Bake for 12-15 minutes or until the pastry is golden brown and puffed.
- Remove from the oven and let cool slightly. Garnish with fresh raspberries and dust with powdered sugar before serving.

Sweets

Ingredients for Lemon Madeleines:

2/3 cup all-purpose flour
1/2 teaspoon baking powder
Pinch of salt
2 large eggs
1/2 cup granulated sugar

1 teaspoon vanilla extract
Zest of 1 lemon
6 tablespoons unsalted butter, melted and cooled
Powdered sugar for dusting

Instructions:

- Preheat the oven to 375°F (190°C). Grease a madeleine pan with butter and flour, tapping out any excess flour.
- In a small bowl, whisk together the flour, baking powder, and salt.
- In a separate bowl, beat the eggs and granulated sugar until light and fluffy.
- Add the vanilla extract and lemon zest to the egg mixture and mix well.
- Gradually fold in the dry ingredients until just combined.
- Slowly pour in the melted butter while gently folding the batter until smooth.
- Spoon the batter into the prepared madeleine pan, filling each mold about three-quarters full.
- Bake for 10-12 minutes or until the madeleines are golden brown and spring back when lightly touched.
- Remove from the oven and let cool in the pan for a few minutes before transferring to a wire rack to cool completely.
- Dust with powdered sugar before serving.

Regency Recipes

INSTRUCTIONS:

Partake in a culinary journey through time, where each recipe embodies the elegance of a bygone era, promising a feast of flavours to delight even the most discerning of palates. Presenting 5 fun recipes!

Regency Era Drink: Wassail

Ingredients

1 quart hard cider
1 cup dry sherry
1/4 cup brown sugar
2 cinnamon sticks
6 whole cloves

1 orange, sliced
1 lemon, sliced
1 apple, cored and sliced
Ground nutmeg for garnish

Instructions:

- In a large pot, combine hard cider, dry sherry, brown sugar, cinnamon sticks, and whole cloves.
- Place the pot over medium heat and bring to a simmer, stirring occasionally until the sugar is dissolved.
- Add sliced orange, lemon, and apple to the pot.
- Simmer for about 15-20 minutes to allow the flavours to meld together.
- Ladle the wassail into mugs, making sure to include some fruit in each serving.
- Sprinkle with ground nutmeg for garnish.
- Serve hot and enjoy!

Vegetarian: Vegetable Pottage

Ingredients

2 carrots, peeled and diced
2 potatoes, peeled and diced
1 onion, finely chopped
1 leek, sliced
1 turnip, peeled and diced
1 celery stalk, chopped
4 cups vegetable broth
Salt and pepper to taste
Fresh parsley for garnish

Instructions:

- In a large pot, combine all the diced vegetables.
- Pour in the vegetable broth and bring to a boil over medium heat.
- Reduce heat and simmer for about 20-25 minutes or until the vegetables are tender.
- Season with salt and pepper to taste.
- Serve hot, garnished with fresh parsley.

Vegan: Mushroom Ragout

Ingredients

2 cups mushrooms, sliced
1 onion, finely chopped
2 garlic cloves, minced
1 tablespoon olive oil
1 cup vegetable broth
1 tablespoon flour (use gluten-free flour for gluten-free option)
1 teaspoon thyme
Salt and pepper to taste
Fresh parsley for garnish

Instructions:

- Heat olive oil in a skillet over medium heat.
- Add the chopped onion and garlic, sauté until softened.
- Add sliced mushrooms and cook until they release their moisture and start to brown.
- Sprinkle flour over the mushrooms and stir to combine.
- Slowly pour in the vegetable broth, stirring constantly to avoid lumps.
- Add thyme, salt, and pepper to taste.
- Simmer for about 10-15 minutes or until the sauce thickens.
- Serve hot, garnished with fresh parsley.

Non-Vegetarian: Roast Chicken with Herbs

Ingredients

1 whole chicken, cleaned and patted dry
2 tablespoons butter
2 garlic cloves, minced
1 tablespoon fresh rosemary, chopped
1 tablespoon fresh thyme, chopped
Salt and pepper to taste

Instructions:

- Preheat the oven to 375°F (190°C).
- In a small bowl, mix together the butter, minced garlic, chopped rosemary, and thyme.
- Rub the herb butter mixture all over the chicken, including under the skin.
- Season the chicken generously with salt and pepper.
- Place the chicken on a roasting pan and roast in the preheated oven for about 1 hour to 1 hour and 15 minutes, or until the juices run clear and the internal temperature reaches 165°F (74°C).
- Remove from the oven and let it rest for 10 minutes before carving.
- Serve hot with your choice of sides.

Gluten-Free: Lemon Almond Cake

Ingredients

1 cup almond flour
1 cup powdered sugar
4 eggs, separated
Zest of 1 lemon

Juice of 1 lemon
1 teaspoon vanilla extract
1/4 teaspoon salt
Sliced almonds for garnish

Instructions:

- Preheat the oven to 350°F (175°C). Grease and line a 9-inch round cake pan with parchment paper.
- In a mixing bowl, whisk together almond flour and powdered sugar.
- In another bowl, beat egg yolks with lemon zest, lemon juice, and vanilla extract until pale and fluffy.
- Gradually add the almond flour mixture to the egg yolk mixture and mix until well combined.
- In a separate clean bowl, beat egg whites with salt until stiff peaks form.
- Gently fold the beaten egg whites into the almond mixture until fully incorporated.
- Pour the batter into the prepared cake pan and smooth the top with a spatula.
- Sprinkle sliced almonds on top of the batter.
- Bake in the preheated oven for 25-30 minutes or until golden brown and a toothpick inserted into the center comes out clean.
- Remove from the oven and let it cool completely before serving.

> Review
> ⭐⭐⭐⭐⭐

Dear Reader,

Did this tome of wit and whimsy tickle your fancy? We are most eager to hear your candid reflections, for they guide fellow literary enthusiasts upon their merry jaunt through these delightful pages.

Leave us your thoughts, be they as sparkling as a well-turned phrase or as cutting as a pointed retort. Your review shall serve as a beacon for kindred spirits seeking solace in the bosom of Regency-era revelry.

Thank you!

Printed in Great Britain
by Amazon